Wanderlust to Wonderful

Kat Martin

Presentation by *BookLeaf Publishing*

Web: www.bookleafpub.com

E-mail: info@bookleafpub.com

ISBN: 9789357617376

First edition 2022

*To my husband, Robert, and three children:
Ethan, Eliot, and Evie. Being loved by you is
wonderful, indeed.*

ACKNOWLEDGEMENT

I would like to acknowledge the writers that sat with me in the late hours of the night from the time I was a little girl fostering my love for books. In the dim lamp glow next to my bed, I never felt alone with the lovely, adventurous, obnoxious, harrowing, frightening words of my heroes: Charlotte Brontë, T.S. Eliot, Ezra Pound, Madeleine L'Engle, Orson Scott Card, Stephen King...The list goes on. I graciously bow to you for your boldness and your pen.

Wanderlust I: From the Start

Creatures of this world starving for creation, seeking the dried up fruit fermenting the soil, already dead and covering the earth with perfume. Its suffocating fragrance blinds them of the new seeds sifting through the wind. Their craving yearns and aches and drives them mad. (Or is it sad?) Bones crack as they feed on the decay. There is nothing left. Emptiness echoes in the depth of their bellies. Keep wandering, creature.

Wonderful I: In the Beginning

An aged hand sinks into the rich brown dirt, cold
from this morning's dew. Lines and calluses,
earth caked creases and dark nails show signs of
the work toiling the mud. It is a gentle
movement, a shifting so loving and sure, little
droplets of sand drifting back and forth, not in
defiance but in surrender. It's a dance, making
room for new life. The seed nestles into the
space which was sacrificed by the old. A blanket
of fresh soil brushes over it, the hand lovingly
caresses the new creation. Will it grow? Will it
be filled with wonder?

Wandering from Here to There, Going Nowhere

Weary wanderer with weathered shoes
Dirty, dank camisoles in brownish hues
Decrepit soles and scraggly hemline
Dragging strips of stained cloth behind

Lonely wanderer with empty arms
Clawing outward through suffocating swarms
Round empty gut, hunger pangs with need
Seek someone to love and ask someone to lead

Aimless wanderer with tired feet
Always arriving to a forfeited defeat
Yearning soul for joy beyond reach
Failing to practice…what is it that they preach?

Wandering to Freedom

I was finally alone, not lonely, but on my own.
The nag of escape, fight or flight.
It was my flight, finally in the air so I could
breathe.
It was my time, 1-2-3, counting up til I was free.
Thinning
thin
air
barely
there
left
me
gasping for breath,
Up high in the sky where I was free to fly.
I let go quickly but kept my eyes closed.
My eyes fluttered
	one eye
		then the other
tears brimming from the light
Why was it so bright up here?

My breathing slowed.
I looked around slowly.
Everything in slow motion.

Dream.
Like.

5

I was finally alone, not lonely, but on my own.

The Wonder of Acceptance

He fell before I knew how much I meant to him.
I never said his name, not once.
(Nor did he, mine.)
Everyone claims dying love a certainty.
But really, it's uncertain if unheard in time.

She tried her best at everything and fought for
her life.
She told me that's how to find success,
Through defeating all the strife.
She held her head up confidently,
while gingerly holding mine.

The others stayed silent and waited for me.
But in that time I grew
Up
Apart
Without. That's all I knew.

Another claimed me in my poverty
a strange acceptance I bear
Ever present
Ever burdened
Ever lifted up in prayer.

Yesterday, I stared in the mirror
Slamming my fist in shame
But in the cracked sharp edges
I began to love, (but what is love?)
the eyes behind the pain.

Today, I picked up the pieces
Of the jagged shards of glass.
Mirror, mirror on the floor
Who can love me anymore?
Just one. And that's the love that lasts.

The Wonder of Time

Is it the long moment before her pinkie crosses
the space to touch yours unexpectedly?
Is it the one second it takes to blink snowflakes
out of eyelashes when she fits into the crook of
your arm to stay warm while playing in the
snow?
Is it the echo of a giggle when you run after her
through the brick walkway, pillars of white
casting striped shadows in the moonlight?
Is it the sliding movement of smooth skin of her
arm, hairless, outrageously soft like satin,
beating excitement through your chest?
What do you count:
the tick or the tock,
the glowing digital numbers robotically
twitching in the dark,
the rhythmic beat of the song playing dully from
an old speaker, or
the breaths in and out of one another's mouths?
Tick. Tock.

The Wonder of Growth

After the ground has been soaked with the
spring rain,
the dirt is left soft.
It sifts and moves and no longer cracks with dry,
cold death.
It births new life in a baptism of colors, stark
against the brown earth.
Deepest ocean blue   Crisp leaf orange
Fresh grass green
The colors ripple out in waves, touching
everything with intention.
A symphony of parts but a whole song, growing
louder.

That's when I breakthrough, wriggling out of the
darkness beneath.
Clawing my way to the surface
an avalanche of dirt rolling off my face

The sun is brilliant in my eyes!
The air is crisp in my lungs!
The wet dew cleanses my fingertips!

Crying tears of gratitude, I hang my head down
in thanks and my hands in surrender.
I suddenly see my feet, clutching the earth in
between my toes.
I gasp for breath in disbelief.
I am strong.

The Wonder of Provision

One toe in, tip toe out
Creeping, sidling, shaking with doubt
One arm reaches toward the shine
Baited breath breathes out "mine"

Slanted eyes slip side to side
Scurrying shuffles in shadows that hide
Gripping long fingers clutch the prize
Saliva seeping out the mouth and cries…

With surprise!

Another gift in plain view
Handed to the creature to make two
As another is piled hand in hand
The hard grip loosens like sifting sand

So much, too soon to even try
Does it wait until the well runs dry?
Or is the well filled infinitely deep,
that this soul can find the rest to keep?

The Wonder of Sacrifice

The vessel waits on the table, empty and expectant for you to come close, to pour into it, so it can sit full bellied while your dry lips purse out every last breath of misty air, lungs starved and deflated, teetering between life and death. And yet, you keep pouring, dripping your life out until you think you can't go on any longer.

That's when they pull up chairs to the table and sit with gathered merriment, fed by your sacrifice. They laugh, drinking more and more, filling their cold hearts with your warmth that you drained so thoughtfully a moment before. When the vessel nears the bottom, you muster up the strength to stand once more and give again. They never even look at you but a glow on their cheeks lets you know that what you're doing is giving life and who would want to allow death to sting? So you pour out again.

The Wonder of Pain

I waited for years, months, days, hours
the stretch of time it takes to sour
the mind, the heart, the soul, the body

it wrinkles

like the grape that dries a dark hued bruise
the sweet purple raisin left to prune
good enough but not enough soon

it buds

until…it was finally time
until…it was finally mine
finally the taste of the winner's wine

it grows

with glowing confidence, I lifted up
giving cheers for the mother's cup
until…the pain that interrupts

it slows

Despite it all…do I dare claim victory?

Am I just blind to what they see?
Are these foolish dreams to speak it be?

it dies

like the raisin dried in the sun
withered away until there's none
just empty dreams to which I run

it flies

.

.

.

.

.

I waited hours, days, months, and years
the stretch of time to melt the tears
to try again despite the fears

it rebirths

The Wonder of Life

Unfurled curl twisted wrought
Stretching the casing until taut
Snapping the thin film, splitting into two
Wide open seed, dark black and blue

Searing like fire, birthing a start
Rhythmic breath for a beating heart
Pulsing river, rushing rapids out
Quickening breath, echoed shouts

And then…
Life is given generously.
And yet…
Will it be kept faithfully?

Soft to feel, yet strong like bones
Coos and gurgles in hushed tones
Fur like skin, shivers when touched
Keep it warm but not too much

Moving brown eyes, what can it see?
Moving swift legs, what will it be?
Moving round bottom, she or he?
Moving my chest, will it love me?

The Wonder of Family

A chubby hand reaches out for the second wooden block, one to pile atop the first that has already been set on the floor before her. She uneasily places it off centered but without wobble, with her left hand. With pride for starting her work, she slinks back to the pile to continue her tower. This third block holds a different shape, cylindrical and skinnier than the squares already stacked.

Again, she raises her arm to gingerly summit the top but her grasp is too suffocating and when she lets go, the entire tower falls with one last breath. Alarmed, she looks up anxiously for answer, for direction, for a reason why she has failed. Instead she is met with an encouraging nod to try again, and though it pains her to think of what once was is no longer, she is determined to succeed.

This time she begins with a semi circle, flat on the bottom and round on the top. She doesn't know that it won't work, but no one stops her, and frustration grows with every attempt to build upwards. They all slouch downward over such a rocky foundation.

In tears of surrender ready to admit defeat, she comes across a flat rectangle. In her last attempt, it works. She adds another, and with each piling block, as she sees the tower grow, a newfound zeal keeps her going. She triumphs with her arms up, a toothy smile erupts upon her face. After the moment passes, she knocks it all down, satisfied.

The Wonder of Friendship

The workers outside toil over the soil gripping
their plows and bending their backs, skin stained
by the sun and shirt salted by the sweat. Their
feet ache with pushing on step after step, and
their fingers callous by pulling weed after weed.
One of them, his shoe has split in half, ripped at
the sole and fraying threads hold it together to
get the work done. It adds to his pain and he
groans in his work. Another finishes his last
drop in his pouch of water, but does so greedily
knowing his future thirst will suffer but at least
his present one is quenched. And yet a third,
exhausted and hungry, grunts out words of
strength and light to his companions. Yes, to get
them to keep moving and finish the work, but
also because he loves them. As the sun slowly
sets in the west, the three stride on, together,
doing the hard work in the field, row after row,
day after day.

The Wonder of Joy

Crunching a crisp red apple
between two bucked teeth
with juice slipping down the corner of the mouth
and its sweet sugar sticky in the palms

Fingering a bright green leaf
dangling from a low branch of the maple tree
with a tire swing gently swaying
to and fro as the children play

Unfurling a new stem as it springs new life
from a seedling below the dirt
with a gentleness that only a mother would have
for a baby reaching up to her face

Drinking the cold, clear water at its source
from the deep well, a fountain unseen until now
with a thirst and hunger for the weary
and all the answers for questions unknown

The Wonder of Home

When I'm all alone and
my eyes shut close
I see so clearly that—

Up on a hill there's a warm log cabin,
with a fireplace glowing full of wood gathered
nearby.
The windows are frosty,
as swelling heat from the hearth
meets the cold air of nature that
abounds and surrounds.
Though the wind howls beyond,
the snow blankets the yard
with a quiet calm,
undisturbed and unheard.
Snowflakes knock gently on the door,
awaiting an invitation.
Just inside the cedar frame,
perched upon the weathered sofa,
an aged face wrinkles with laughter
at the little ones romping around the room,
singing joyful songs of youth and play.
Smells of spiced meat and sweet pies
roam the home,
bringing yearning to the grumbling bellies.

In anticipation,
he bellows with a deep baritone
that it is time,
like a pleasant bell ushering the feast.
She brings forth a platter,
kneaded and heeded
with her love and her time;
the whole lot of them
gather round in hunger.

—and then suddenly,
my eyes flutter open
and I carry the warmth of that dream
for as long as the day will allow.

The Wonder of Purpose

Moving forward like a rushing brook
One step at a time
Down stream
Down stream
Down stream

Looking backward like a skipping stone
Slaps, splashes, sighs
Drowns.
Down.
Down.
It sinks.

Stopping still like a strong root
Wavering like dancing.
Pushes.
Pulls.
Stand your ground and be silent.

Facing upward like a stem
Crystalizing in the sun
Drink.
Soak.
Dry the tears

Braving onward like a fresh wind
Breathing and living
In.
Out.
Filled with wonder

The Wonder of Submission

Floating on your back
down a cool stream
on a hot summer day
with the sun shining and
just enough clouds
to shield your eyes
so you can gaze
upward at the white shapes
lazily drifting by
and at the shelter of leaves
from the trees lining the shore
waving casual hellos
with every calm breeze
small splashes cool your face
while your fingers slowly trace
the movement of the river
that dances around the rocks
with each turn you trust
that you will be kept safe
in the water's full embrace
as it carries your frame
in the natural refrain
a rhythmic ebb and flow
not knowing what's next
or where to go nor why

but it's not drowning yourself
when you choose the dance
to joyfully surrender
and float on your back
down a cool stream
on a hot summer day

Wanderlust II: At the funeral

At the end, they crawl on skeletal frames with eyes sunken into blankness; the dry dusty wind ripping through their flesh, not like a lion eating its prey with satisfaction but an infestation that consumes slowly until the death that they denied throughout their entire journey from here to there. What made them most human became their assassin: always lusting for more, craving for something else when the beauty was always right in front of them. The realization is maddening. (Or is it saddening?) The haunting wasteland of dreams unfulfilled becomes a graveyard full of ghosts wandering onto eternity.

Wonderful II: After death

The farmer sighs with relief that it is over: the hard work that required much of him. It nearly broke him. (Or maybe it did.) The digging down deep into depths that were unseen just to find the perfect sand for his seed. The weeding of overgrowth, of undergrowth, of the beautiful and painful wrongs not made right. The watering that poured out, gushed out, spilled out everything he had left. The pruning that broke his heart to see taken apart in order for the new to grow. The harvesting that called out to him at dawn, his head barely up from his pillow, til dusk when his eyes fluttered shut in exhaustion. It is done. There is rest. There is peace.

And then the next season comes, and the farmer gazes out over the new rows of tilled soil, breathing in the fresh smell of wet dirt.